"*Advice to 9th Graders* is painfully beautiful. I was pleasantly surprised by the level of emotions evoked as I read. The words focus on some of life's greatest lessons that we often are not taught but unfortunately stumble upon. I felt the magic of the words seep into my soul."

—Dr. Shanell Sanchez, Associate Professor, Department of Criminology and Criminal Justice, Southern Oregon University

"It is no small feat to create a safe space for tweens and teens living with the impacts of incarceration. To then hold and read the gift of their expression in such a beautiful package is an honor for all of us."

—Amy Cheney, juvenile justice advocate and librarian

"Maya Angelou once said, 'There is no greater agony than bearing an untold story inside you.' This sentiment perfectly captures the essence of the remarkable collection of stories in *Advice to 9th Graders*. The advice shared not only is riveting and powerful but also has the potential to transform lives. This book is an absolute must-read."

—Tige Charity, CEO and Executive Director, Kids in the Spotlight

"What struck me most about the teenage writers in *Advice to 9th Graders* is their unconditional and uninhibited honesty. They don't just give advice. They chart a path past pain and betrayals as they acknowledge their own struggles with shame and identity and belonging. Their greatest message is their example: 'We got through it and you can too. You're not alone.'"

—Diane Lefer, author of *Out of Place* and, with Hector Aristizábal, *The Blessing Next to the Wound*

"Another soulful, weighted bundle of truth and dreams encouraged, gathered, and curated by POPS. This collection of stories and poems feels like a rite of passage from harm to hope, which is something we all need. Whatever has come before, it is not the sum total of what defines us. There is so much possibility ahead."

—Jonathan Zeichner, nonprofit founder and leader,
    Los Angeles

"These raw and vulnerable voices may be young in age, but their piercing insights reflect hard-earned wisdom through their unique experiences and perspectives. They will beam a light through your mind and heart."

—Karin Gutman, founder of Spirit of Story, Inc.

"May the voices in this anthology move you to amplify their stories to promote narrative change and galvanize around the critical future-building work to improve social and economic well-being for our emerging adults."

—Erica King, Senior Manager, National Resource Center on
    Justice-Involved Women, Center for Effective Public Policy

"Incarceration, detention, and deportation can be deeply isolating experiences. POPS the Club publications combat that isolation with community and conversation. In *Advice to 9th Graders*, young people speak directly to each other, advising and affirming those with shared lived experiences, while informing and enthralling those who don't have those experiences. This book fills a void, shines light into dark corners, and provides hope in the most unexpected moments."

—Lauren Marks, author of *A Stitch of Time*

"The artists and writers of *Advice to 9th Graders* have given us an incredible gift—reflections and representations that stir the heart and mind and remind us that wisdom, hope, and grit arise when we lean into life's beauty and chaos and dare to share our journey and insight. The youth behind this beautiful anthology are timeless teachers offering perspectives that can move each of us, regardless of where we sit in life."

—Alyssa Benedict, Executive Director, CORE Associates,
    and cofounder of Women's Justice Institute

ADVICE TO 9TH GRADERS

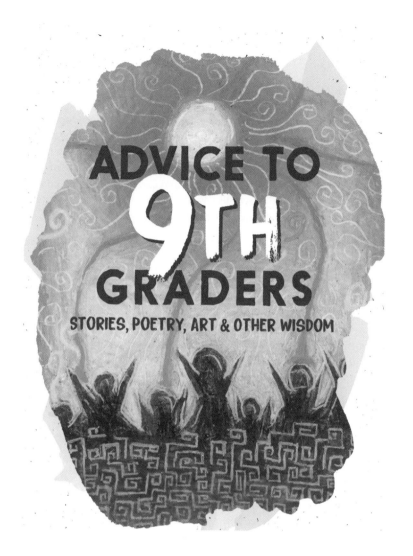

ADVICE TO 9TH GRADERS

STORIES, POETRY, ART & OTHER WISDOM

A PATHfinder and POPS the Club Anthology

Out of the Woods Press

Out of the Woods Press
www.outofthewoodspress.com

Quantity sales. Special discounts are available on quantity purchases by corporations, associations, and others. For details, contact the "Special Sales Department" at the address above.

Orders by US trade bookstores and wholesalers. Please contact BCH: (800) 431-1579 or visit www.bookch.com for details.

Printed in the United States of America

Cataloging-in-Publication Data

Names: Friedman, Amy, editor.
Title: Advice to 9th graders : stories , poetry , art & other wisdom / edited by Amy Friedman.
Description: Portland, OR: Out of the Words Press, 2024.
Identifiers: LCCN: 2023915111| ISBN: 978-1-952197-14-7
Subjects: LCSH High school students--Literary collections. | BISAC YOUNG ADULT NONFICTION / Family / General
Classification: LCC PS508.S43 .A38 2024 | DDC 810.8/09283--dc23

First Edition

Cover designer: TLC Graphics
Editor: Amy Friedman
Interior designer: Reider Books

"My Palette," Giselle Montiel-Laconna

Things change. And friends leave.
Life doesn't stop for anybody.

—Stephen Chbosky, *The Perks of Being a Wallflower*

Contents

CONTENTS

CONTENTS

CONTENTS

CONTENTS

CONTENTS

CONTENTS

CONTENTS

Introduction

We both feel grateful for the opportunity to introduce *Advice to 9th Graders: Stories, Poetry, Art & Other Wisdom,* the first anthology from The PATHfinder Club (Paving a Trail of Hope). This book carries on the tradition established by the eight POPS the Club anthologies preceding it. The PATHfinder Club and POPS the Club have become one, and this is our first publication together. A quick recap as to how we got here, a vision that became a reality.

Victor:

I sat lonely in a California prison cell with a life sentence, but I still had a vision. I visualized seeing a brighter future; I visualized not wearing prison blues; I saw myself wearing my own clothes, looking professional, facilitating youth-led groups. Loneliness and the fact that my father had been incarcerated throughout my childhood couldn't erase my vision. A life sentence couldn't steal my vision. I was destined to obtain my freedom, destined to mentor youth and to help them pave a trail from hurt and harm to hope and healing. I was granted parole in November 2020!

Jess:

Seven hundred miles away from Vic's prison cell in California, in Portland, Oregon, another vision was being created. The Pathfinder Network (TPN) was dreaming of a sacred and special place where teens could be in community with others just like them and pour it all out (or simply listen), in the hopes that together they could create something powerful. We wanted to do more with teens who we knew were suffering, because we had been those teens, and we know how important this support is. Driven, passionate, and eager, each with their own lived experiences with systems, came together, supported by Amy Friedman and Dennis Danziger, founders of POPS the Club and our guides and light. And so The PATHfinder Club (TPC) was born.

With the support of individuals who have been impacted by incarceration, detention, and deportation, we launched our first PATHfinder club in May 2022 at Parkrose High School in Portland. Nine months later, in February 2023, POPS clubs from California, Georgia, and New York joined our team. Since the first club meeting in Portland, we have been honored to provide a safe and nourishing space for youth impacted by the same systems that have impacted us. We wish that when young people close their eyes, they don't have to envision a life different from the one they are currently living. We wish the hurts we hold in our hearts, minds, and bodies weren't the same ones that so many young people are holding in theirs. We wish that there was no shame or stigma surrounding their experiences. We wish they didn't have to hide their truth.

Still, we are so glad to be able to support these young people. Whether they live in our neighborhoods or miles and miles away, we want every young person to know that others are thinking the same thoughts they are thinking, feeling the same way they feel. We want them to know we are here to honor the truth behind their words and their visions. We are here to ensure that their truth is never silenced in the ways that ours were.

This book is a testament to the excellence of those minds and the truths of each of you out there.

Victor Trillo, Jr., and Jess Sandoval
The PATHfinder Club Facilitators
The Pathfinder Network

"Pathfinders," RG

IT ALL GOES
BY SO FAST

*Life moves so fast. You gotta
document the good times, man.*

—Big Boi

"The World as You Make It," Chelsea Robb

Poetry

Sara Ivonne

My empty mind is my empty page.
It's almost like a cage.
A cage that is locked with all my thoughts,
So they won't go flying across.

My mind sparks.
I remember my remarks.
I jot them down in such a rush.

Now, let me discuss.

Everything is transient and so are you

Jimmie Harmon

i have these fleeting moments of freedom
points in time where i'm soaring
They're always fleeting but the feeling
lingers, i can't place why or how they come
about, but it's freeing, like i've been living
wrong up until this point
i strive for this feeling daily but i've yet to bring it back

Fulfillment

Anonymous

Be open to change. Everything around you will
constantly change, and sometimes you cannot
control it. I've found that while in high school,
I learn new things about myself every day, whether
from the people I meet or things I experience.

This is truly a fulfilling journey.

Leap of Faith

Sara Ivonne

In life
It's crucial to jump.
Whether it be in
the swimming pool
or jump rope.

The leap of faith
is what we need.
It's petrifying but
it gets the job done.

Two Fresh Perspectives about Entering High School

Oliver Green and Selma Bahy

Oliver:

Entering high school, I was eager to thrive in a rigorous academic environment. Everybody talks about high school as some horrible place where teachers fight you on any minor disturbance, but this isn't the case; most of the time, teachers genuinely care about you and try to make a difference in your academic journey.

I can't reiterate this enough: If you have questions, you need to ask. It's not embarrassing. It doesn't make you look stupid. It is necessary.

Grades are important, always keep that in mind, but take it from me, a student who spent the last year and a half stressing whenever my grades dropped to 98 percent, grades aren't everything. They're important, but personal happiness is far more meaningful than your six different percentages.

Make sure you study for important tests, but it's okay to get a B or even a C on exams. You'll feel better about yourself and your academics if you take care of yourself first.

Another aspect of high school is the social side of things. Find two to three good people who you can truly consider close friends, and the rest should be others that you know and like well enough to get together and hang out with outside of school.

Social anxiety might also loom over you like a giant shadow, and I know this is hard to swallow, but once you stop caring what others think, things get better; you'll feel more confident about yourself, making it feel like things are finally falling into their correct places.

Finally, the classes you take are important, and rigor does matter—although, after excelling in freshman year, I was expecting sophomore to feel like a breeze, and it is anything but that; AP classes aren't called Advanced Placement just for the title. They are no joke and seriously require a lot of time and effort. If you aren't in the best mental headspace, I don't recommend taking more than one serious AP class, but if you feel confident in yourself and your mental capacity, challenge yourself if you are up for the challenge.

Overall, it's important that you form meaningful bonds with your teachers so that you can eventually ask four or so of them for letters of recommendation; these are helpful for getting into colleges of your choice. Also important: forming meaningful bonds with your friends so that you can determine who you truly do or don't want to be around and who makes you feel like the best you and the happiest you. Finally, form meaningful bonds with yourself; trust and prioritize yourself.

Good luck with entering high school.

Selma:

One of the best pieces of advice I can give you is to please remember who you are. As you enter high school, you will see people and situations that were once familiar to you begin to change—and it's scary. It's terrifying when people and things in your life that always comforted you begin quickly changing, but the best thing you can do for yourself is to not lose touch with your hobbies, your aspirations, your moral values, and who you are as a person. You should never change an aspect about yourself simply for the purpose of appeasing others.

I understand that is much easier said than done. I am a people pleaser myself, and it becomes so incredibly draining to constantly try to cater to everyone's needs because of some impulsive feeling you have to do so. I always thought it sounded so stupid when people told me to never change for anyone else, but being a second-semester sophomore now, I realize the things people have been telling me are real. Remembering that you yourself are the only person you will always have by your side is something that is not only an underlying theme in high school but in life in its totality.

Something I don't think anyone candidly prepared me for as I came into high school is the sheer degree to which academic rigor increases. Even as a child, I put a lot of pressure on myself during middle school and elementary school to achieve the best grades possible on my work, due to my upbringing as well as my own motivations and goals. Despite this, though, I remember being told that middle school grades didn't matter, a notion that served as something of a lifeboat for me. If I didn't do well on a test—well, it was okay. My grades didn't ultimately contribute to my future, so there was no issue. As soon as I had reached high school, though, a wave of harrowing realizations that my true academic record had begun pummeled me underwater and drowned me. I was no longer in the shallow end of the ocean; I was in the middle of it, during high tide. I don't think a lot of people put enough thought into just how abruptly you are thrown into freshman year.

I know a lot of you reading this are probably fresh out of middle school, and, in the most direct way possible, I would like to tell you to begin thinking about freshman year. I would like you to think about what classes you may be interested in taking. I would like you to think about what friends you want to keep around and if you would like to branch out and meet new people.

Two Options

Tamira Shany

You have two options:
Take pride and fail.
or
Endure and succeed.

Everything Will
Be All Right

Imari Stevenson

Time flies, so hold on tight.
You live and you learn
But make things right.
Focus on yourself and hold on tight.

Make some mistakes
But not too many.
You're in 9th grade now,
So be ready.

Lots to learn,
Lots of growing
Stay strong, and hold on tight.

BE YOURSELF

Don't hide yourself in regret,
just love yourself, and you're set.

—Lady Gaga

Biased Comparisons

Rachael Galper

I advise incoming 9th graders not to change themselves to fit the expectations they feel from those around them. These are the years of their life to find their true, authentic selves and to express that without fear of judgment.

"Biased Comparisons," Rachael Galper

Somewhere between Then and Now

Jess Sandoval

Somewhere between then and now silence became loud.
Anger turned to understanding,
Loneliness turned into comfort,
And dandelions aren't just weeds.
Somewhere between then and now my will to live for
    others turned to the will to live for me.
Somewhere between then and now I started pouring into
    myself the way I always had for them.
Between then and now I stopped thinking about a world
    without me and imagining what the world would be
    like with me in it.
And somewhere between then and now I started to fix
    the parts of me that I never realized were broken.
I started to pick apart myself before others could.
Somewhere between then and now soft skin turned to
    calluses.
Somewhere between then and now the rain feels good on
    my skin.
And tears don't bother me when they roll down and drip
    off my chin.
Somewhere between then and now I have changed, and I
    think it made them change too.

But I don't wait for it anymore.
Somewhere between then and now I had to move along
the path alone.
And sometime between then and now I made myself my
home.

The Big Picture

AM

- Minor details don't matter in the big picture.
- Watch how the people around you treat others; they could treat you the same way one day.
- Even though it may be tedious, focus on your work. Half of the things that matter to you at this very moment won't matter in 10 years, trust me.
- Don't waste your time on something that's not your passion.
- Don't burn bridges; it might end up hurting you later.
- Although it may be fun to have lots of friends, don't trust people easily.
- Find something you love; it can help the hard stuff not be so tough to work through.
- Relationships aren't everything, but if you do find the right person, try and stick with it as long as it makes YOU happy.

Don't Be Afraid

Nico Romero

Don't be afraid to say what's on your mind.
Keep yourself composed. Don't be
stressed about what's next.
Just work on what you have to do now.

No Te Decaigas Sé Fuerte

Lisbeth Vásquez

Sé fuerte no importa por lo que estés atravesando
sé fuerte nada es permanente todo
es temporal cada cosa pasará
y en algún momento de tu vida mejorara
no te deprimas pues
tú haces de tus días
lo que tu quieres que sean
aprovéchalos vívelos sonríe
vence tus temores
llora si tienes que llorar si tienes
que hacerlo saca lo que llevas dentro
pero jamas decaiga
pues en esta vida no
tendrás carga mayor
que no puedas soportar

Don't Give Up Be Strong

Be strong no matter what you're going through
be strong, nothing is permanent but temporary
everything will pass
and at some point in your life it will improve
don't get depressed
you make all of your days
what you want them to be

take advantage of them, live them, and smile
overcome your fears
cry if you have to cry
doing that brings out what you have inside
but never falter
not in this life
will you have a greater load
than you can stand

Advice to My Younger Self

Estephanie Lopez

Advice from POPS

Going back to 9th grade, I think of a lot of things I could have done, should have done, and would have done if I weren't so afraid about what other people said and perceived me as.

I think the best piece of advice would be to be yourself, genuinely. Not trying to please other people just because you want to be liked. People say that it is most important to not get on anyone's bad side, and although that helps, it is not ideally what will get you through all of high school. It really depends on the situation and the way you feel about that particular person. Make sure you are confident enough with yourself and take time to make that happen if it is not already something you luckily possess. Once you achieve that, you will have a much better relationship with the world around you.

- Stay true to these four agreements from Don Miguel Ruiz's *The Four Agreements*:
  - Be impeccable with your word
  - Don't take anything personally
  - Don't make assumptions
  - Always do your best

May God bless you! I am sending a lot of hugs and kisses
Sincerely, Estephanie Lopez

Where I Come From

Anonymous

I come from a home that is broken,
I come from wanting to help myself before others,
I come from wanting to have an answer for everything,
I come from wanting the best option,
I come from too many paths,
I come from a noisy mind,
I come from me.

Two Steps Forward

Davi M. R. Cavalcanti

There's an expression people have: "Sometimes you take
two steps forward, then one step back. And vice versa."

But sometimes when you are far from everything
you know and are accustomed to, it looks like you
are taking one step forward and seven steps back.
Sometimes it seems like everybody is saying
you are doing everything wrong.

But in those times know you are just doing it the
way you know, the way people do things in the place
you come from, and now you are in a different place
with different people who don't understand you.

Who Am I

Shakira Gomez

Who am I
I am Shakira Gomez
Is that who I am
Am I just a name
Want to say something else, but my tongue just twists
Twisting into a new person every day
Finding myself trying to untwist myself

I am someone who is from
hard work, dedication, and determination
Taking the phrase *ponte las pilas* seriously
Being competitive toward everyone
Feeling like life is a competition

The walls in my house, the floors and the roof are the
    foundation of me
The walls I grew up drawing on
The floors I would walk on barefoot
The ceiling I wished to touch one day

Growing up being close to my neighbors
Feeling like everyone in the building is a part of my
    family
Running around with others
Knocking on people's doors, laughing and running away

Senior Advice

Paulina Luke

To the incoming freshmen and other underclassmen:

To be completely honest with you, I have no clue how I ended up being the one to give advice to you. Because it feels like just a moment ago I was in your shoes, trying to get through my first years of high school by dragging my tiny feet across endless hallways.

And then some dude across the world ate a bat, and the next thing I know, I'm back at school with size 11 shoes and only one year left to walk these hallways. And then the next thing you know, I am weeks away from leaving this place forever, and you expect me to give you some valuable advice (which we all know is just a code word for "I did this—don't do it"). But we all also know that you are still going to do it, no matter what.

So instead of telling you what to do, I'm going to tell you how to do it. And unlike Fight Club, I only have one rule, and you can talk about it (even with women).

Scientifically speaking, I might be a physics-over-chemistry advocate for life, but if there's one thing I must admit about these two subjects, it's that chemistry beats attraction. Every. Single. Time.

And I'm not just talking about your stupid hallway crush, but wherever you go, whoever you meet, and whatever you decide to do, always go for chemistry and not mere attraction. Plain attraction is often superficial and one-sided. Chemistry, on the other hand, is genuine and reciprocated.

Don't do something because other people make you think it's the right thing to do—that's attraction.

Whatever you do, do it because it makes you feel something in return and makes your life feel worthwhile. Do it because there's chemistry—but also accept that not all chemistry is here to stay, and sometimes you're better off letting it go.

So, by now you are probably thinking, "You still told me what to do." Yes, yes, I did. But you know what? I'm the one graduating high school, and you are probably younger than *Grey's Anatomy*, so maybe by the time the show is over you'll be old enough to write your own Senior Advice.

For now, buckle in, because high school is going to be one hell of a ride—a turbulent one, but unlike what Hollywood makes you think, not the ride that defines the rest of your life.

Poetic Advice

Donaji Garcia

Poem 1: Advice of a Parent (Part 1)

I may not know you
Nor you know me. . . . But just know
You are valuable
You are loved
I want you to succeed
I trust in you
And you should trust in yourself. Please trust me.
Trust the people that love you.
You can find me in these pages.

Poem 2: Advice of a Parent (Part 2)

High school can give you the tools to prepare yourself
I know that not all of you might want to go to college
For most, we would love for you to go
I do know that dreams can take you into new directions
Please eat your meal
You got this.

Poem 3: Advice of a Peer (Part 1)

I have some grandmotherly advice for you.
If you are seen as different
Use that to your advantage
Some might feel the same way
And on those rainy days
Remember that you are strong
You have the potential to make a difference.
You can be the first.

Poem 4: Advice of a Peer (Part 2)

I had my heart broken in high school
And my sister had a life-changing surgery.
There are people who face challenges
And when storms form ruffles through your skin,
I hope you find an umbrella of a person to support you.
I know I did.

Poem 5: Advice of a Sister (Part 1)

I am scared too
It is my first day at a school I have only seen in pictures
Why can't classes be online, right?
Where I can have home-cooked meals
And do exams with my pjs on
Just remember that it is not only your first day
But others' too.

Poem 6: Advice of a Sister (Part 2)

I can promise your grades will give somersaults
Your heart will have many butterflies and you might be
    confused
No worries, it is due to enamorment
Embrace high school
You will be surprised how much personal knowledge you
    will have
You can see why you are so special
As always.

Three Years Ago
I Wish I Knew . . .

Gizella Huertas

That high school isn't all about grades but your
experiences and the people you meet.

I wish I knew
it's okay to struggle and a bad grade
isn't the end of the world.

I wish I knew
to be involved with school, whether it's
joining a sport or a club.
It is one of the easiest ways to make friends.

BE YOURSELF

Be kind to your teachers and treat them like humans too.
They are giving you an education with
their time and effort
And if you're friends with them,
they can be more lenient on you.

Finally, I wish I knew to be myself.

YOU'VE GOT A FRIEND

Friendship . . . is born at the moment when one man says to another, "What! You too? I thought that no one but myself . . ."

—C. S. Lewis, *The Four Loves*

VIDA MUELLER

"Light," Veda Mueller

Guide to Friendship Making

Feven B.

- Find people who you can be yourself with
- Take time to interact with people
- Dress well
- Make a good impression on people
- Don't make enemies
- Join clubs, reach out
- Don't do something you'll regret later
- Practice mindful awareness, think about your actions
- But don't always focus on friends
  - remember to focus on yourself

Don't

Akinn Solis

Don't get into stupid relationships.

School Isn't the Entire World

Kennedy Johnson

Make friends, join a club, start playing a sport.
Do anything that will help you make friends.

It is so important that you have a strong support system
to get you through school. Forming bonds with anyone,
even a teacher, will make school much more bearable.

I also advise you do something you feel passionate about
(outside of school). Something that helps you escape.
That way, when school feels overwhelming, you have
something that reminds you: School isn't the entire world.

Pretending

Anonymous

To all future freshmen:

Find people you can be yourself around.
Don't be with people you need to pretend around.
Make good friends, because they'll help
you through the worst days.

Finding Home

Andrea Phoebe Orduña

For the first time in my entire life, I have found a
place as comfortable as home, regardless if these are
the welcoming arms of Cali, Salina, or Kai or the
conjoined laughs with Evan.

Ever since I was a little girl, I have felt like the
princess locked in a castle, far from civilization.
If you asked me what the best part of my year has
been, without a second thought, it was finding
my friends in The PATHfinder Club.

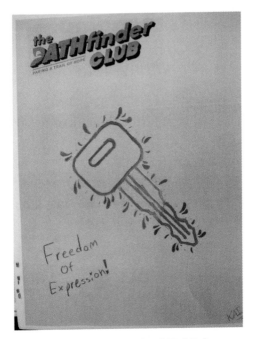

"Freedom of Expression," Kai Salazar

Advice about Friends

Kai Salazar

Don't f___ with fake people!
Don't let people tell you who to not be friends with.
Hang with YOUR group, not someone else's.
Be who you are, don't let someone change you to be like them.
People will talk sh__ about you regardless
So, have fun with what you do
NO SHAME!

Changes over Time

Ashley Villatoro-Gomez

Dear incoming freshmen,

I'd like to let you know some things I wish I had been told before I entered high school.

First of all, don't rely on friendships.
I'm not saying you should stop being friends with them, trust them, or anything above those lines for that matter. But sometimes you just have to focus on yourself.

Trust me when I say this:
Most of the time friendships you build will likely end, but that's just from my personal experience.

Eventually, you'll find new friends with whom you can build new connections and memories.

Involve yourself. Building more friendships is a huge advantage, since you'll have them to support you whenever you're in need of it.

And give yourself breaks. School can often be overwhelming, and you may just feel like giving up, but keep a positive mindset instead and give yourself the time you need as long as you're putting your best effort into what you want to be and to become as the years go by.

Watch Out

Tyler Stonebraker

Watch who you hang around with or call your friends, because they may be quick to use you. I learned to keep the ones who are closest at a distance.

The Do's and Don'ts of High School

Kavon Ray

Don't hang around with the wrong crowd. You know who
    they are.
Don't run to the lunch line. If you run, you look like a bot.

Do play sports or an instrument.

And join a club. And if you're afraid to do it alone, go
    with a friend.

Friends Have Your Back

Will

What comes to my mind is being here for my friends who
are here with me and are always here beside me so that
nobody will hurt me or harm me or touch me.

I'm happy that my friends always sit by me and have my
back, everywhere I go.

They will always be with me.

Friends Make the Difference

Leo Acosta

I'd like to tell 8th graders this: Make friends.
I'd like to say: Don't be scared to interact with people

And focus on school because once you mess up, you'll have
so much to catch up on.

My freshman year, I messed up. I'm in 11th grade, and I'm
still doing freshman year work, trying to catch up.

EMOTIONS IN MOTION

It is only with the heart that one can see rightly; what is essential is invisible to the eye.

—Antoine de Saint-Exupéry, *The Little Prince*

"This Old Dog," Roslyn Chamale

It Started With

Krystle May Statler

the door	*the door*
of a	*of a*
church he	*car she*
walked through	*sat in*
officers came	*men ran*
they shot	*they shot*
he ended	*she ducked*
with two	*as two*
bullets inside	*bullets flew*
one kissed	*one burst*
the temple	*the window*
then he	*then it*
became ash	*became diamonds*
the other	*the other*
went through	*went into*
a wall	*the door*
did he	*did she*
see the	*sense the*
bullets coming?	*bullets coming?*
officers watched	*officers watched*
the blood	*the breath*
flow from	*flow from*
his mouth	*her mouth*

ADVICE TO 9TH GRADERS

brother		and	mother
share	the	same	nose
the	same	almond	eyes
almost	the	same	autopsy

Collaborative Piece

Kay

We were the last two people on earth, but we couldn't speak the same language. We learned to sit in silence and live in each other's presence. We communicated with our eyes and appreciated each other's touch on earth, when we felt our love unearthly.

Home was not a place but a person, and the feeling we held together. I felt nothing but warmth looking into their eyes in dual solitude, someone who I began to see as my safe place. Someone that lit up the world's bare emptiness. I began to think this is what love is, what it feels like. How it could be so simple if we take off our masks. We fell in love, with each other's vibrations, despite all odds placed against us, and my soul found its way back to you, as if we were the last two people on earth.

Justifications of War

Malikiah Ozment

Life is as influential as peace and war
All it takes is one flicker or flame
To ignite pain
People say peace would end all war
But the truth is
Life would be too simple if there were no conflict
Conflict fuels our economy
War brings in good money
While causing others to suffer
Take this to heart
Never live in the dark

Don't Love

Nathan Pugh

Years ago, I saw a girl shining like a star.
At the moment I did not see it.
Once I got to know her, years later,
She changed right before my eyes.
Like lint accumulating in a dryer vent,
When I saw her before I didn't care.
Love and happiness are what she receives.
She loves and loves, but no,
She doesn't love me
For I am an amazing guy to her but just a friend.
I do not define love to her.
Love at first sight is a lie.

"Sea Foam Dreams," Stephanie Santiago Garcia

A Dream

Jimmie Harmon

you run through the maze that is my mind
leaving stained handprints and distant
laughter, forever cementing yourself into the
crevices

i had a dream once
i lived with you and we had a detective
agency
i want to do stupid things and solve crimes
with you forever

"What Is This?"

Avel

What is this
Feeling,
Like my heart being ripped out
Everything is spinning and I can't
Breathe
I need to breathe
I lost all feeling
Numb

I'm shaking
I look at that poem
I'm suffocating, but no matter what I do
It
Won't
Stop
Please stop
I can't do this anymore
I won't do this to myself anymore
What is this . . .
"love"?

Tears

Avel

I find myself lost in the maze
Of memories, it's like a trap, a trap of
Sorrow
Do I hate
You? Do I love you?
I miss
You,
Who are you?
I knew nothing about you
You never shared a tear
Or sang your sorrows
Like the morning sparrow
Stranger who shares memories
Memories of love, more
False love than another
You're a stranger whose words ring in my head
A stranger who loved another yet did not realize

"The Energy of Flowers," Hailey Garcia Garcia

Four

Jimmie Harmon

Energy

we are both energy
we intertwine and intersect
like parallel twine trying to meet

Beneath

there is something deep beneath my skin
it festers in the silence
itching to get out
clawing at my inner workings
begging to be let out
begging to be paid attention to
begging for me to acknowledge it
but i won't

Weapon or Flower

emasculate me
tell me what a man doesn't do
is my body meant for love or for labor?
is it a weapon or is it a flower?

Sunspots

the sunspots in your eyes
you said she's pushing daisies
i cry helplessly at your side
she's a ghost in training
sleepless nights
absent lights
unbearable days
grand finale

Silent Anger

NM

Anger, an emotion I commonly feel
I feel this anger when I think how pathetic I am.
Angry because of my teenage hormones.
But also, what makes my blood boil is the thought of the
    mistreatment me and my siblings went through with
    my mom.
Angry and resentful for my father who left me to feed
    his addiction but also for me not thinking I was good
    enough for him to stay.
I was not good enough.

I'm angry at the fact that I can feel these unbearable
    human emotions.

My anger is so loud, but I stay silent.

Why? Because of her
To prevent myself being a spitting image of her
So I suffer with this silent
Anger until I erupt like a level 5 volcano
With my anger, sadness, irritation.

By the Sea

Kay

You come to mind when i look at the sea
You were all i wanted to be
So i took your name
shared each other's pain
But in the end you are who i have to blame
For i don't know if this is heartbreak or addiction
You have caused me both
with the illest intention
Our songs were just my delusions
you were this perfect illusion
Meet me by the sea
on August 16th.

Your Senses

Anonymous

Enjoy this trip, 9th graders
There's so much to see and smell and hear and taste and feel. . . .

I Know

Avel

"Who are you?" Who am I? I have many answers . . .
But I just know
I like the color purple,
I know my favorite food is spaghetti when it rains,
I know I like the fall, it has my favorite holiday,
I know I wish for someone to get me flowers
because as a kid I always loved them,
They were my only desire.
I know I stay up at night just to see the stars,
And I know that someone out there is
looking at them too.
I know I like to have stuffed animals around me
because it feels like I'm not alone
When I'm scared, I know it's taboo,
I know I stay to myself because I don't want
others to feel sorry for me when I weep,
I know what it's like to feel lonely but to
be around a crowd,
I know I give too much of myself, but it's
okay as long as others are happy
I know who I am
I am . . .
The girl who's learning to know herself

Freewrite to My Sobriety
This Is Our Goodbye

Kay

You made me feel euphoric, and for that I chased you
instead, you caught me, and I have to let you go.
I longed for some happiness and warmth,
you made everything go silent, you made me feel numb.
I chose you, I chose this feeling that fooled me.
You never took me to bliss.
I open my eyes and I regret picking you
choosing you
Because you've consumed me
all my thoughts, all my feelings
my consciousness
The moment i consumed you.
I can never hate the things I've loved most
But you
have changed me, in the worst way.
I hate myself for choosing you, time and time again,
substance cannot take my pain away,
when I'm sober my guilt finds you.
I am not an addict
I cannot be my father
but when I looked in the mirror,
I had cried for the last time.
You made me feel shame, this caused upon myself.

ADVICE TO 9TH GRADERS

I will always yearn for forgiveness, mine above all else.
How could I let you have a hold on me like this
I am leaving you.

I am choosing me.

I hate you, for breaking me.

The War of My Thoughts

Avel

Who I am is not a hard question
I am me that I will mention
At times it does start to
Make me question
Who I am
They ask me
"What are you thinking?"
Deep down
I'm thinking of
The emotions I hide,
Of the anger I keep inside
The envy I have of others' lives
I think of just how I've always
Dreamed to fly
I think . . .
I know myself, right?
I find myself in love with others' lies,
Share a part of my heart with a rhyme
Even tend to help others to find their spark
Speak their mind
Love their heart
But I think I'm
Falling apart
What if they're watching
Every move and breath
Waiting for me to crumble
Waiting for a wreck.

My head is filled with sounds that are bound,
Bound by a broken song,
Songs with a torn melody
I can't think for
Myself
Who am I?
A person who is falling apart or
One who helps others love their hearts?
Maybe I am just someone
At war with her thoughts

Demons . . . a Rant

Owen Brookshire

Demon (noun): An evil spirit or devil, especially one thought to possess a person or act as a tormentor. A cruel, evil, or destructive entity.

I think demons are more widely accepted as spiritual entities, but I'd like to offer a different perspective on demons. I think I'd work the definition a little differently—something like a past decision or regret coming back to torment you. With this definition, I think a lot of people have demons.

I want to introduce you to mine so we can have a basis of what they are for me. They are always lurking in the background of every day and every decision. It could be a small voice, an urge to indulge in a vice, or a desire to throw everything to the wind and do whatever I want. But for every one regret or bad choice there are more—which means you must learn to live and prosper with the demons who live in your head.

Anger is a demon that can be very destructive but can allow people to do good when used properly. It's a high risk/high reward scenario. If you choose to lock up your anger, you can use it to protect people who can't protect themselves. But if you don't take the correct precautions, you will lash out at people you don't intend to receive it or who don't deserve to be punished for your inability to control yourself.

Find the strength within yourself to manifest a cage for these entities. Snuff out their flames, and choose when they can breathe. Just because you have demons doesn't mean they're in control. If you neglect them, they grow stronger and can completely unravel your progress. To help relieve the stress, you can call for help. Ask for their help in making better bonds that last. Two minds are always better than one. Just remember, you are always in control. You always have a choice. It's only when you don't give them the choice to come out that the demons win.

Never let someone or something else make a decision for you except when you don't have the knowledge to make a wise choice. I once gave them control, and my body has taken the toll for that. My scars have scars.

Demons are malevolent creatures. You should never allow something to control your emotions and never suppress your emotions. Doing so removes what you can bring to the world and takes you away from those who can love you. In the end, if left to dwell, the demons can destroy you, but you can become stronger if you use them.

Thank you for listening to my TED Talk, lol.

Suffocating in Peace

Avel

I'm encased in water in the deepest part of my ocean,
Starting to panic,
Trying to get out,
I'm desperate to get out
My arms damaged from trying to swim up,
Legs I can barely feel . . .
I'm suffocating
Everything and nothing is all around me
The dread I feel knowing
No one will save me.
No one at all
I stopped struggling, ready for the end,
Expecting my end, but
I'm still . . .
Alive?
I'm in the deep
I'm in the quiet
My mind is undefined
No one's around to hurt me or condemn my thoughts
No one's around to see me suffocating
In a way it's peaceful
Drowning in the deepest part of my ocean, floating in the
    middle, and maybe it's temporary
Even so
I'm no longer scared to suffocate

Blessed by You

Kay

Love's beauty is infinite
Itself is never-ending
It is vibrational and it is safety
It is known the moment two souls meet
So how can I love you
Something that is bound among us
a euphoric feeling that is easily made between energies
is forever unattainable between you and me
Our eyes will never meet again
The ones you have created on the soul you couldn't raise
Drink me away, and when you close your woeful eyes
Grieve the daughter you chose not to love.

Pain to Motivation

Tyler Stonebraker

No money for rent, my mom stressin',
smoking weed to try to get it out of her head.
She doesn't deserve all the pain she has to go through.

One day I want to get out of poverty.

Pain, it's a deep feeling of hopelessness
that can break you, but you gotta use it as
motivation, or it can eat you alive.

Hate

Avel

All I can think is
Hate,
I hate you and how you make me
Feel
Why feel this way?
Why end this way?
All I hear are her words replaying
"We laugh, scream, and sing like silly little kids, hoping we
don't accidentally sin"
Repeat
Repeat
Repeat
In my head I scream
Your feelings weren't for me
But for her . . .
Her
Maybe you hoped I was her
Maybe you were with me to get over her
So now I sit here
Hate controlling me
I hate you
And I hate that I ever loved you
"I wished it was you"
He put his hand on my face
He looked me in the eyes and told me
"I still love you."

He loves me?
After all this time . . .
As our lips touched
I felt his body get closer to mine,
I felt his hands connect to mine,
Smelling his strong cologne
In that moment
I wished it was you
I wished it was your soft lips touching mine,
My warm hands connected to your cold ones,
Your warm body closer to mine,
You have the specific scent of clean laundry
and a light cologne that reminds me of only you,
Your hypnotizing eyes
looking into mine,
Telling me you still love me
As I opened my eyes, I saw him and in my head I hoped it
     was you
I put on a smile trying not to cry
And told him
"Me too"
"For every flower."

You were not my first flower
My first flower hurt me with its thorns when I tried to
     help,
My second flower used me to keep its petals from falling,
My third flower was with another,
My fourth flower made me wait six months and left me
     when I needed that flower,
My fifth flower disappeared and I could not find it,

And you
My sixth flower
Were the one that hurt the most because
You were a real flower,
Whose thorns pierced me
Not letting me get close
So for every flower
I lost a petal
I am now a stem from a flower that wilted
Yet a stem can grow into a flower again.

TO YOUR HEALTH

*You can't run away from who
you are, but what you can do is run
toward who you want to be.*

—Jason Reynolds, *Ghost*

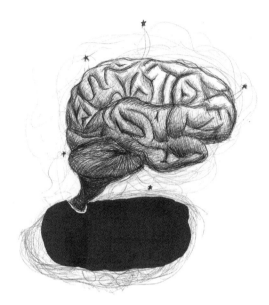

"Choices and Changes," Tamira Shany

Choices and Changes

Tamira Shany

The brain represents our minds, thoughts, and, some could go as far as to say, souls; its logical nature juxtaposes our feelings we express at POPS every week.

Incoming freshmen should understand: They have to have common sense and keen learning abilities to navigate the new high-school world. The black abyss under the brain is an element holding many high-schoolers back, representing depression, anxiety, delusion, and what could come about from those distasteful thoughts and actions.

Going for It

KWL

High school: football games, homecoming, friend groups, superlatives, relationships, prom, and graduation. In reality, is high school the same as the way it is portrayed in Hollywood?

Based on my first two years of high school, many aspects are similar to movies and TV shows. For example, in a majority of public high schools that have a student government, they usually have a multitude of activities like homecoming, bake sales, prom, and football games to increase school spirit. Something that is not always expressed is the stress, anxiety, growth, and trials and tribulations that many high schoolers experience throughout their four years.

Ways to help prepare you and get you through the "trauma" people call high school is to honestly take everything one step at a time, one assignment at a time, one day at a time, even one social interaction at a time. And don't forget to breathe. I know it may sound cliché, but breathing actually does work.

An easy way to start hating school is to not pace yourself with the amount of work you receive. Pacing yourself with work, friends, family, self-care, and hobbies is a great way to reduce stress.

I have had a difficult time finding a balance within life, and I know if you are learning how to follow a good pace, YouTube videos and clubs that offer study skills may help you. As long as you work with your teachers, complete your assignments, spread kindness, not start/stay out of drama, look for the positive things at school, you will be okay, and you will probably enjoy high school!

Try your best to take part in what you love that the school offers, like clubs, sports, art classes, student government, dance, and theater. Attending school events and dances is another great way to get involved. Whatever you may be going through in your life or whatever people tell you, remember, always follow your goals.

Everything is possible if you believe and go for it! I understand that this may sound way easier than it is. Don't let society's standards or stereotypes tell you what you can and cannot achieve. If you want to try cheerleading, try it out! If you have always wanted to run for class president to make a positive difference, go for it! It is not always easy to get out of your comfort zone, and it is not mandatory whatsoever to do so to get through high school, but pushing is a good way to build more community, meet new friends, and if you are struggling with life's purpose, it may help you realize it.

Whatever you have done in the past does not define who you are tomorrow/in the future, so go for it!

And at the end of the day, remember that high school is only a portion of your life.

The Future

Bonnie Loborico

In the future I want to be a lawyer. I want to be able to help people with their problems. In the future I want my family to be a bit big. I'd like a husband and three beautiful kids. Being a mom has always been a dream. I want to be able to travel the world and visit new places with my big family. The places I'd like to visit are Paris, France, Hawaii, the Grand Canyon, and most of all California, because I've heard it's a beautiful place.

I'd like to have a garden in my yard, with a farm. I want to live in a big house with a lot of room for my family. I'd like three big dogs.

I'd like to be appreciated even if I have a disability.

Everyone Needs Help Sometimes

Amori Storms

I would like to live a life where I'm not worried all the time, a life where I have a consistent schedule, a stable job, good people, and an accepting/accessible environment. I wish I could do more for myself, and most of all, I wish people didn't look at or treat me differently for needing help. Everyone needs help sometimes; I'm hurt that needing help is such an issue specifically because my body is literally structured differently from other bodies.

Having a space where I and other disabled people can just exist and ask for assistance without being judged or treated differently is my ideal world.

Above and beyond, I dream of having accessible healthcare. It would be nice if all disabled people could go to a doctor, tell the doctor, "This is what's happening," and be taken seriously and listened to. I wish mobility devices weren't so expensive.

Dream Life

NM

I would like to have a comfortable life. I want a life where I always have enough money. I want to live the life where I can work my dream job. That's the life I want—to be able to do all of my hobbies. I want my dream home with a family and the person I love. I want to have my dream wedding and wedding dress. I want to achieve all of my goals. My dream job is to own my own business and upcycle houses. And I kinda want my own cafe.

Making My Mark

Kai Salazar

I want to leave a mark on everyone I meet. I want to share a little piece of myself every time someone talks to me. I want to be so crazy famous that people talk about me for hundreds of years. I want someone to cry tears of happiness after seeing me because I changed their life.

If I'm not famous, I want to live in a beautiful meadow where it's basically spilling year-round with kids and animals. I want to feel like a little farmer. I want to have my hands filled with dirt by the end of the day. I want to help my kids wash their hands. I want to have them play with farm animals and goats! So many goats! I want my spouse to scold me because I took the kids to go watch the stars at midnight. I want my hands to bake amazing goodies. I want to read books by the fireplace while my kids sleep.

I want to have a beautiful daughter who will have dimples just like my brothers. She'll be a genius and will always correct me even though I hate it. She'll have soft skin on her arms and rough hands. She'll be amazing, and I will be proud of every single thing she does. Man, I am so scared of ruining kids but that's all I want—a daughter who is some part of me and the rest of her. I want to see her grow into herself and figure out her passions and interests.

I want to have a healthy, loving family. I was so f'd up as a kid, and I was dealt some horrible cards. I would have done anything to escape the constant drug-ridden world I was living in. I want to raise children who aren't scared to ask for food. But I don't want them to ask for food, because they won't have to: It will already be there. I want to help them with their homework and not make them cry. I want them to feel overwhelming love every day. I want them to show that love to other people. I want to be comfortable and successful and I want to love someone. I want to be scared of life but continue living it. I want to end the cycle.

I want to be different from my family.

Abstract Advice for a 9th Grader's Future

Maxwell Poll

- None of this matters (even though it may seem like it does). Despite this, at the same time, this period of your life is integral and will shape the remainder of your life in compounding ways. So try your best to act according to these two contradictory ideas.

- Don't waste time on things that don't help you achieve your goals.

- Find an impactful but achievable direction that you want to lead your life toward and push at it. If you can't do that, at least think of people, fictional or real, that you would like to be similar to, and strive toward their ideals. Still, Do Not Imitate.

- Study history: This is not the first or last time that what you are experiencing is happening, and remember:

  - "The only constant is change." —Heraclitus
  - "The only true wisdom is in knowing you know nothing." —Socrates

- Sometimes we feel like we have no control over our current situation. Contrary to this, however, when we think of time travelers, we believe that even the smallest action or interaction they have with someone in the past can massively affect our present.

You are that time traveler, living today.

To the Previous Versions of Me

Valerie Contreras

Dear freshman me,

It's me, Valerie. I'm you from the future. This letter is to all my past selves. I'm writing to you as a senior. High school can be scary, but it can also be one of the best memories you will create in life. You will prepare yourself to become a young adult, and you will learn many lessons as you go on with your life. You will learn to let go of things, because most of the time they aren't worth holding on to. I have learned my self-worth and how to let go of people who aren't healthy for me. It can be a little difficult to know how to differentiate between healthy and unhealthy when you have love for them. But nothing in life is really easy.

It's okay to be confused. Don't think you are supposed to get everything right the first try. . . . Life is all about trying again and not giving up.

Sincerely,
Future (better) you

Forward

Lyric Farmer

I was closed off once
I accepted my status as
I was systematically placed in
A stereotypical stigma
That I am just an uneducated, face-tatted, junkie criminal
Who is fettered and bounded by recidivism and an
Incarcerated lifestyle
Then I began to realize all the real lies
Hopefully. Not too late
That there was a possibility
A chance to change my fate
To not be a statistic
But an exception
To be accepted in more
Than just society today
By putting words into motion
Creating an action plan, if you will
I went against all odds
And against the grain, just to gain
That education, and career
To be a voice worthy to hear
Making a vow that I won't quit, bend, or bow
To anything or anyone that is of the oppressor
or oppressed

ADVICE TO 9TH GRADERS

I will not be impressed
Or distracted from my destination that I have set
I am an advocate for myself
I am not what the labels say I am
I will push and persevere
Through all of the pressure
Even if publicly I am ridiculed
I will claim that power of knowledge
In changing, I will establish myself and
Apply the skills and tools
Utilize my resources and move forward
Education is my token
When one door closes
Another one opens

It's Okay to Not Be Okay

Nimran Singh

Life is going to hit you like a roller coaster.

The next four years will be nothing like *High School Musical*. Sure, there will be good times. But there will be the most dreadful times as well. And that's okay. People change, and so will you. Watch your mental health, it's the most fragile thing about you and can easily tear down in high school. Anxiety is okay, stress is okay, and sadness is okay. Being alone and wanting time away is okay. Everything you're feeling and will feel is valid, it's okay. Mental health doesn't have an end, it's an ongoing battle. You may feel like you're trying, and trying, and trying, and nothing changes. Like you're stuck in a deep hole with no hope and no help.

That's how I felt for the majority of my freshman year, and I still feel like that sometimes as a sophomore. Depression isn't something to take lightly.

Make sure you find key connections with people. Surround yourself with people who make you happy; don't try to fit in with the cool kids. Stay away from the people that focus on their image more than their character, the people that tear you down, and the people that don't make you happy. Make sure you don't invalidate what you or others are feeling and

going through. Everyone is facing their battle,
you're not alone. Keep your head up and talk to adults
for help. You can face this, I know you can.

And whatever you do this upcoming year, don't give up.

WE ARE FAMILY

The bond that links your true family is not one of blood, but of respect and joy in each other's life. Rarely do members of one family grow up under the same roof.

—Richard Bach, *Illusions:*
The Adventures of a Reluctant Messiah

"Riding the Waves," Hailey Garcia Garcia

Don't Push

Tyler Stonebraker

My advice about family is to keep them close,
because sometimes they're the only people who
will have your back. Don't push them away.

I've seen a lot, and for those who don't have a family,
reach out to friends, counselors, or teachers if there
is anything you need to talk about.

I come from a broken family, and it's always been
just my mom, my brother, and my sister.

Don't Let Them Stop You

Kai Salazar

Don't let family stop you from being YOU.
You're beautiful, kind, and intelligent!
Sometimes your birth family don't know that.

Whoever makes you feel loved is your family.
Don't limit yourself to blood.
And family, blood or not, will be complicated and may
    hurt you at some point.
That's part of growing.
No one is perfect.

Empathy and Mom

Jaden Saetern

Visited my mom after about five months, and it was nice
to see her, but I knew she was stressing and having a hard
time settling in with new people and without me and my
brother.

The Best

Will

I love my family who go to school where I go,
Parkrose High. I want to let them know they are
the best. They support me in everything I do.

Encourage friends and family members to join
clubs and sports and other activities in high school
and bond with their fellow classmates.

Your Own Thoughts
and Feelings

Amori Storms

It's important to remember that above all else,
no matter what happens, you're a person
with your own thoughts and feelings.

Communication is vital. Make it clear where
you stand and how you feel about the things
people say and the ways that they treat you.

Your family should treat you with respect. And always
remember, blood doesn't make family, relationships do.

Dad

Kai Salazar

Big arms tattooed and bruised
A smile filled with white crooked teeth
A blue durag always on
Someone taking pictures for my first day of school
Big fingers I could wrap my hand around
A scratchy voice from years of smoking
A voice I'll never hear again
Arms I will never get wrapped up in again
A smile I will never get again
A blue durag I'll never get to see him wear
First days long gone
Fingers wrapped around needles instead of my hands
A dad who was there every day turned into a memory

Tears Don't Fall

Shay

I hate being mad and sad, it just makes me more mad. There are a lot of feelings I hate, but the worst feeling is salty teardrops running down your cheek into your mouth while blue and red lights flash in your face. Teardrops running down while the cops put your mother into a cop car.

Teardrops running down while you remember her saying she was here to stay.

Teardrops running down while you hold on to your dog plushie, your aunt taking you into her house where you will live for another two years, maybe more, maybe less.

The tears stop for a while, and then it's the year 2020.

Tears come and go while you see your mom abuse drugs and alcohol. She hates being mad, but she seems to love being mad at me.

I was once her little innocent pretty princess, but now I'm a little stupid negro.

Year 2022, tears don't fall while you walk into your apartment that once had a door. Tears don't fall as you look at the broken door the cops busted down.

Tears don't fall as you hear her voice for 15 minutes as long as her books are paid.

Tears do fall as you listen to similar stories people tell that make you realize the fake smile you've had for years.

What Do I See Day to Day in America?

Billy Mendez Trujillo

People don't see the struggle
People don't see the injustice
People don't see what we go through day to day
People don't see when we help out
People only see what they want to see
Why is it always us behind bars?
They say we live in a free state
They say we matter
They say they want to help
They also say that we are all equal
They say it is not black and white
Who you see filling up the jail cells?
It's always been our culture
It's an African American
It's a Latinx
It's people of color behind those bars
I don't see the police harassing white people
I don't see them going to jail for stealing
I don't see them going to jail for hanging out in groups
They even made a group named the KKK
Who do I see behind those bars?
I see my culture getting divided

I see less and less
All they want is to live free
All they want is to help their families
All they want is to feed them
All they want is health care
All they want is better opportunities
All they want is to put a smile on their kids' faces
All they want is for their kids to have better lives
All they want is for them to live without a worry in the
    world
All they want is a second chance
All they want is to fight back and get treated equally
All they want is for their kids to have the best life and not
    to worry about being themselves
    everywhere they go
I try every day and do not give up.
I try and won't give up. Why stop?
If each day you get misunderstood
Each day they don't treat you right
Each day they talk down to you
Each day they say they care
Each day they say they will give us a second chance
But yet it doesn't stop there
They want us all behind bars
They don't want you to see the truth
They don't see our side
They don't see what we go through
They don't see what we have to do to eat.
They don't see our hard work or appreciate it.
I say f___ it. Why? Because I am not trying to be a slave
Yes, I work, but yet I get seen as a criminal

Now, is that fair?
Where do we go and get food?
Where do we go and get health insurance?
Where do we go and get that help?
Where does the food you guys don't eat go?
We still see people dying of starvation
We still see people in the streets without homes
We still see the injustices that happened each day
They just want free labor workers
They want to get rich and not help
They want us to give our humanity up to them
They think we are disposable
They don't want to help us
They should help us prosper and care about our health

TEACHERS AND GRADES AND HOMEWORK, OH MY

*One child, one teacher, one book,
and one pen can change the world.*

—Malala Yousafzai

"Drowning in Paperwork," Penman*by Caerulea*

ON GRADES AND HOMEWORK AND OTHER SCHOOL WISDOM

Define Yourself

Sara Ivonne

It's sadly funny
that many
let a single grade letter
define them.

It's only when we look deep
into ourselves
and who we truly are
that we learn that a lot of things define us.

To Graduate

Will

Work hard.
Get y'all work done on time.
Turn it in for your teachers to check it for you
so your grade can look better.
If it's an A or a C or a P, y'all are going to pass.
You'll graduate and get your diploma.
You can go to college and become what
you want to become.

Be That Person

Cherry

Some advice to 9th graders:
    Always do your homework, no matter what
Never procrastinate
Never miss out on activities
Make sure to try your best, and make sure you make good
    friends
Even if you don't make friends, you're just starting . . .

Ninth grade for me was the most interesting year
Although there was work, you'd sometimes be rewarded!
Never skip, or go with bad influencers
It doesn't make you "look cool" whatsoever
Do things that are good for you only

Don't be somebody you aren't—that'll lead to chaos in the
    future
Just because you see something that everyone else is
    doing, don't do it
Unless it's something that benefits you in a serious
    situation

Help others, be that person
It's not embarrassing, just don't let them get possessive
    over you

ADVICE TO 9TH GRADERS

Always HAVE boundaries
Be nice about it

Always raise your hand if teachers ask questions, or "Can
    anybody tell me . . ."
Never be distracted, no matter if it's your friends
    distracting you

If you make a friend and you always wave to them, but
    when they look at you they don't do the same, leave
    them
They don't care, so why are you going to think they're
    going to be there when you have problems
If they don't care about you

Be a good influence on other kids, never look for
    problems just because
It does not look good on your resume

Make sure to join activities that are available
You'll regret it later if you don't!

No Free Pass

Alphonsine Mbuyi

There's no free pass. If you fail, you will repeat
the grade. So don't trip when it comes to
school now that you are here.

Grades

Zaleeyah Ross

Wassup, 9th graders,

Honestly, we are losing hope in the future generations
(class of 2026 and below), but you guys need to prove us
wrong!

Focus on your grades, they're very important. When I was
in 9th grade, my mom always reminded me how important
my grades were. To tell you the truth, I always lied to her
about them. I'd tell her I had made all As when really, I
had a bunch of Cs. My self-confidence was very low, and I
felt self-conscious in class. I never raised my hand, never
asked for help.

And that took a horrible toll on my grades.

I could no longer take the suffering, and I turned my terrible fall grades into amazing As in every class. I had a 3.66 GPA. And that changed everything.

Grades are important and will give you a boost of self-confidence.

Rolling with It

Jonathan Gonzalez

If you get an F or D in class don't stress about it, because you'll get nothing done. Instead, just roll with it and study more and get help from your teachers.

Ninth grade is going to be really easy, but it gets harder as you get into 10th and 11th.

Try to take an AP class your freshman year because it will help prepare you for future classes. Take Honors Chem your sophomore year. Try to get all your A-G requirements done as soon as you can so your senior year is easy.

Time Flies

Anonymous

High school is shorter than it seems.
Don't be afraid to ask questions.
Take breaks while doing homework so you don't get
    burnt out.
It's okay if you don't feel like socializing.

Your Homework

Kai Salazar

Don't put it off, try and do it as soon as you can. Give yourself breaks too. Listen to music. Don't be afraid to ask for help. Surround yourself with a good environment. Do what works for you, and also, f___ homework, it was invented as a punishment.

Homework on Your Homework

Feven B.

Don't procrastinate
Take notes (good ones)
Be organized
Stay focused
Less screen time
Don't get distracted
Study

Take Responsibility

Daphne Colio

"Beginning of the new year, it's a fresh start—what could
ever go wrong?"
Those exact words are what you tell yourself the very
first month of school
Little by little by little, school gets harder
At first you tell yourself, "Do all your work; have good
grades; don't mess up."
Then you get tired and start procrastinating
And then, little by little, your grades go down and you
gotta bring them up.
Near winter break, and beginning of second semester, it
changes
That saying that you tell yourself at the beginning of the
year, it changes
So now it's saying "Pass with Cs & up; don't procrastinate;
get through the year."
Your grades go up, so now you feel a little accomplished
and you tell yourself
"I'm good for now, I can take a break."
You're doing great for a few weeks, you don't have to
worry
And there you go again, all the procrastinating comes
back, and your grades go downhill.
Now your grades are Ds and Fs and everyone tells you the
same thing
"If you keep this up you won't pass my class."
"Get your sh___ together, you need to pass."

"I know, I know." It's your responsibility to do this
So why aren't you doing anything about it?
The year is ending and you're rushing to finish every little
    assignment
Slowly, very slowly, your grades go up, you stop
    procrastinating
Everyone has that one person who brings them up
Telling you, "You can do it. Finish strong. Don't give up
    on yourself."
They give you that bit of hope that you can ACTUALLY
    do this.
So, you believe them, you don't give up, you try to
    accomplish everything,
You try to not let them down, not let yourself down
Everything's coming together, you're passing your classes,
    you don't have to worry anymore
At least not until next year, I mean you've learned your
    lesson this year.
Haven't you? Take responsibility. Don't Procrastinate.
    Don't Mess Up.

Perfection, the Enemy of Good

Laine Riley

9th graders,

Your lives are about to change. High school can be really fun but it can also be pretty difficult. Now is your time to be social, make friends and grow. Get creative with clubs and sports.

Don't be afraid, and if you're going through a tough time, ask for help from teachers and counselors. The people at school want to help you.

And if you only take one thing from this, turn in all your assignments.

Perfection is the enemy of good, and you can easily become overwhelmed.

Procrastinating

BL

Homework and its subsidiaries are extensive and -also short. You need to do it, but do you want to? Your friends are talking or messaging you. Procrastinating is okay because friends are important too, but you need to learn to procrastinate better.

Understand that the future has more weight than the present and that homework is a simple key to a good future. Each assignment adds an ounce to your future's worth, yet if you don't do it, it takes away a pound.

It's okay to procrastinate. Just get better at it.

How Much Money to Bring to School

Savannah Brewer

Bring at least $2. Everything in the vending machines
costs $1.25, but a bag of chips the same size
only costs $1 at the Student Store, and you'll
need an extra dollar if you want a drink.
So, $2 is useful for a bag of chips and a water.

How Much Money to Bring to School

Kennedy Johnson

On an average day when you come to high school,
you should have $1.25. You can buy chips at
the Student Store for $1. If the store isn't open,
you can buy snacks at the vending machine for $1.25.
Don't bring more money, because it is easy to
want to spend too much on food.

ON TEACHERS

Respect

RG

Show respect to your teachers, because they hold great wisdom that will be passed on to us, and we will pass down that wisdom to the next generation.

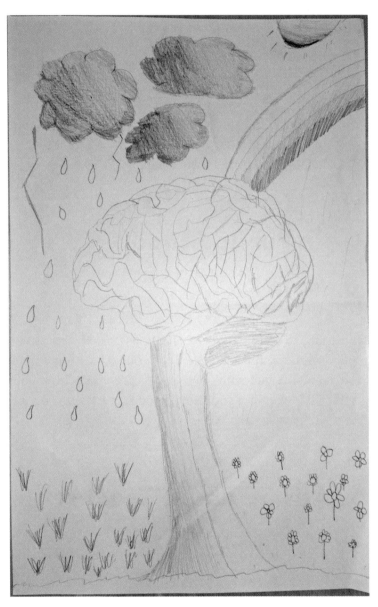

"The Duality of Nature," Maxwell Poll

Difficult and Kind

Anonymous

Some teachers can be difficult, and some can be kind
and generous.
Either way, treat them with respect.

In Public School

Kavon Ray

One thing to know about teachers is this: If you attend
a public school, most teachers let your education stay in
your hands. If you show you don't care, that's how your
grade will look. But if you show you do care, then you most
likely will earn good grades.

Advice about Teachers

Akinn Solis

Match their energy!

Empathy

Tyler Stonebraker

Don't give your teachers a hard time; some of them don't want to be there as much as you don't want to be.

And they don't get paid enough for this!

Reading Rooms

Raymond Pacheco

Be observant. Learn to read the room and
your teachers. And don't be
shy or scared, because all of your teachers
have been in your shoes at
some point, and I do believe that they care.

On the first days of school, have manners and be polite, and for the first few days, when you come to school, be observant. Go to class and meet all your teachers and talk to them. Make friends with them because, in the big picture, if the teachers view you as a friend, they won't let you sink. They will talk to you and give you feedback on how to pass their class.

TRAVELING FROM HERE TO THERE:
ADVICE ABOUT TRANSPORTATION

*Lots of people want to ride with you
in the limo, but what you want is someone
who will take the bus with you when
the limo breaks down.*

—Oprah Winfrey

"Traversing the City," Hailey Garcia Garcia

Don't Stress It

Amori Storms

Learning to take public transit isn't hard or a big deal,
But look up the route on your phone if you haven't memorized it.

Don't be afraid
But be cautious—if you set your bag down, put your leg in a strap to keep it close.

Always be aware of your surroundings.
But don't stress it.

Public Transportation

Kai Salazar

Don't be afraid but be cautious about public transportation. Especially if you're a woman and/or POC.

Keep yourself safe and try to travel with friends. Memorize your way home.

ADVICE TO 9TH GRADERS

I like walking and taking the bus because of how cool it is sometimes.

I hate the bus when it's crowded, but when the bus is empty, I like it because I feel like a main character.

Deeper Meaning

Andrea Phoebe Orduña

Burn everything you love, then burn the ashes.
I struggle to find the deeper meaning of that simple line.
The deeper meaning of things, maybe I overthink, over-
exaggerate the things as soft as silk. I always search for a
dent in fixed findings.

I have grown fond of trains. I hear the rumbling of concrete
crashing against the rocks and see the nostalgic shimmer
of sunlight kissing your skin.

Be cautious! Not everyone is as they seem.
Before you let down your guard, trust your gut!

Some things aren't worth risking your life for.
Disinfect after using any public transportation.

Don't Be Afraid of the Bus

Tyler Stonebraker

This week has been better. My mom is no longer mad at
me and she will start work again soon.
We all wait for better days, but sometimes
you gotta go out and get it.

One day I want to be able to buy a Ford Mustang.

For now, don't be afraid to ride the bus!

Eyes Up

Drake Witham

Keep your eyes up and off your phone.
The world is much better entertainment.
And always have something to read.

"A Walk through My Home," Yulissa Gonzalez

ADVICE TO MY FUTURE SELF:
The Callaway Middle School Kids

When did you start to forget how to fly?
—Chance the Rapper

"Market Run," Yulissa Gonzalez

ON GRADES

Get Those Grades Up

Jamal

Don't mess up. You only got one more year, so get your grades up if you need to, and don't give up. You have people who want to see you succeed. Don't mess that up for them.

Do Your Work . . .

David

Do your work. You need better grades.
And remember this:
Although you are doing well in school,
this won't get you anywhere near
your goals.
You need to be healthy and do things
so your brother can't hurt you.
Even if it seems hard to reach your goals,
try your hardest.
Don't give up, carry on with your goals.

Your Transcript

Alex

Pretty much every college will see your grades from the first year of high school as part of their transcript review. Even universities that emphasize 10th, 11th and 12th grades, when they evaluate applicants for admission, they see those 9th-grade marks. This is the year to cement your fundamental skills and build your confidence to move on and have a successful high school experience.

The Future

Qua

Go ahead and figure out what you are going to do in life. And make good grades! Also, do good when no one is watching, and never give up on your dreams!

Separating School from Home

Jordan

Don't let your grades get down because of things you do. Don't let things from home affect you at school.

ON TROUBLE

Keep Going!

JJ

Go to school every day. Do not be late to class or school. Keep going! Do not give up. Keep going when times get hard. Keep going! Be nice to others and meet new people, and you'll have a better school year. Keeping going! Do not, and I mean do not, be bad to a teacher, to other students, or to other people in your school.

Be Prepared

Jacob

Always be prepared for things in this life. Don't let things get under your skin. Try your best, in life and sports.

Stay Out of Trouble

Maximus

Stay out of trouble and keep up your grades, because colleges will look at your grades. You could get a free ticket to college, make it in the NFL or NBA. So keep up your grades and you'll have a great future. Keep life right, and you will be good!

Letter to My Future Self

Bradley

Do not get in trouble. You need to find the right people to hang out with and do your best in school. Never give up. When you get your first car next year, do not wreck the car. Take care of it. Do not be an instigator when people get into fights. Try never to watch them.

Good Recognition or Bad

KaeKG

Do not get into trouble, because high school is not a joke. You need to focus during classes if you plan to go to college. High school is preparation for college. I know a lot of people want to be in the NFL and the NBA and things like that, but you don't have as many chances as you used to. High school is not about playing and getting into trouble. People will recognize you for who you are and for what you do. You'll either get good recognition or bad, and that's your choice to make.

Dear Future Self

Naya

Listening to the wrong people will get you in trouble or left behind. Following the wrong people will get you to where some of the things you want in life you won't be able to have.

Stay to yourself. Take that JROTC class you want, and take it for three years so you can get those credits. Stay in marching band. Do the things that keep you focused.

It doesn't matter what anybody says about what you're doing. Do what you want to do!

Try doing the things that make you happy. You know how you wanted to swim against people? Do it! If you don't like it, then move on.

Help keep people smiling, and if you ever need something and nobody can help, just remember your scripture: Jeremiah 33:3: "Call to me and I will answer you and tell you great and unsearchable things you do not know."

The Wrong Crowd

Cookie

It can be tough throughout life, but you have to do well in life and school. If you hang out with the wrong crowd, you will end up in jail.

Dear Future Self

Corderiana

You are on your way to high school. Keep going and never give up. Stay out of trouble and get your grades up, and keep them there! And try out for the step team, and push yourself.

Good Students/Bad Students

Ethan

There are good and bad students at your school. The good students have good grades, good behavior, and they're nice. The bad students are the ones with the bad grades who do bad things.

Be good.

Think Before You Act

Bella

Everyone knows not to drop out, or at least we're
all told that. But to be honest, I think you
shouldn't drop out because it's not smart.

Stay in school, finish so that you can get a good-paying
job. Stay motivated, and don't do bad things.

Think before you act, please.

Going to College

Noah

Hello, fellow 9th grader, stay out of trouble, and do not do
drugs. Find good people to hang around with and tell them
not to do drugs. Stay in sports. Stay healthy. Never give up
on what you want in life. When I get my first car, I will be
able to go wherever I want, and I'll go to college.

In Your Ear

Akerria

Keep going, you got this. Focus on yourself.
Don't let anybody get in your ear.
Go with your first mindset.
Make sure you've got a good friend group.
Be positive and love yourself, even when no one else does.

No Bullying, No Trouble

Amiriyah

No getting in trouble, and no bullying others.
If you want to try out for a sport, push yourself and do it.
Don't get pregnant, you're too young for all that, and I'm pretty sure you don't want to have a child at 15 or 16 years old.

Keep Your Head Up

Brookelyn McGownse

Hey, I know it's rough to be in high school.
You have all that pressure on you.
You can fight through this. It gets better.
Just do well in your classes and listen to your teachers.
Don't get into fights.
Don't pick a fight with anyone.
Believe in yourself and keep fighting to the end.
You got it.
Don't give up.
Keep your head up!

Girl/Boy Mess

Bailee

Don't get into a lot of girl/boy mess.
Don't get into fights.
Don't be friends with toxic people.
Don't start drama.
And be kind.

ON SPORTS

Dear 9th Grader

AP

I hope you can try out for the softball team. Just know
    you can do whatever you want.
One thing I learned is to never give up on your dream.
The next thing: Never give up on your dream.
And last: Never think someone doesn't love you.
Someone always does.

A Sport for Everyone

Bryson

When you're in 9th grade, you can try out for
sports—
Basketball, football, soccer, track, because high
school might be boring without sports.
And if you're a girl, you can do track and
basketball, volleyball and more.
Playing sports is fun!

You Just Might Like Sports

Emberily

Choose your friends wisely, friends with a similar personality to yours, and don't let the teacher get to your mind. Just do your work and stay calm.

You might be interested in playing sports, so do what you like. Whatever you are interested in, you can do it.

Basketball, Baseball, and Track

Jaxsen Hudson

Don't drop out of school.
Never do drugs and things like that.
Never let your friends pressure you.
Try out for sports.
Try basketball or baseball.
Try track.
And don't vape.

My Future Self

Donovan

Make sure you do your work and stay in school.
Make sure you try out for the basketball team!
Stay consistent.
And don't get in trouble.

Softball

Abby

I hope you can try out for the school's softball team.
Just know you can do anything you want.
I learned never to give up on your dreams.
I learned never to put yourself down, even when times
    are tough.
I learned never to think nobody loves you.
Someone will always love you.

Wrestling

Larry

To my future self:
I want you to stay in school and get a scholarship.
I want you to keep wrestling in 9th grade.
Wrestle until college so you can be good.
Stay in school so you can do something in life.
Don't hang around with the wrong crowd.
Be good in school.
I believe in you.
Stay in wrestling!

NEVER GIVE UP

Never. Give. Up.

Kenny Jung

Hello, 9th grader.

I hope you are doing well. I hope you have good grades. I hope you are living a good or wonderful life, and I hope you have something you like or enjoy doing. I'm sure you're a smart person, with academics and with yourself. Please be mindful of yourself, your family, and the one or several things you like to do.

If you like sports, or anything else, just have fun and enjoy yourself. If you're serious about it, never give up. Keep working hard.

I used to play soccer for fun and nothing else. I wouldn't try my best, I just played around. I even almost gave up on soccer. But I thought my parents would be disappointed, so I kept playing, and at some point I decided to do my best to become one of the best soccer players in the world (not yet).

Now I'm still playing soccer, still doing my best, but I'm also having fun with the sport I love.

So just have a good time and live a good life and work hard on something you're serious about. Never. Give. Up.

Walk Away

Jax

Stay in school and pay attention in your classes.

Be a good friend and make sure people you hang out with are good people and don't want to do anything bad or put pressure on you to do something bad.

Don't do drugs or vape outside or in school. Keep your health good.

If somebody creates conflict, just walk away. Settle the problem without fighting.

And try to do after-school things to keep you busy.

Think

Calleigh

I know high school is hard, but stay outta drama! Focus on your grades and not on what everybody else is doing. Make sure you stay with the right group of kids. And when you get a car, take care of it, those things are expensive!

To stay out of drama, THINK BEFORE YOU SPEAK.

Peer Pressure

Emily

Peer Pressure. It can be tough, but you gotta keep going and push through. Be your own person. Don't listen to what people tell you to do. Sometimes a situation is complicated, but you have to stick to what feels right for you. Don't let people push you around or control you. Stick up for yourself. Be who you are.

No Fooling

e5lei

Try your best to stay in school and make your family proud of you. Don't be in the streets. Stay in football. I hope you and your friends stay close. I hope you get all that you want.

And don't let the girls fool you.

Hellcat

Smoke

Graduate, keep your grades up, stay
out of trouble.
And get that Dodge Charger Hellcat
you want.

Try Your Hardest

Jaxon

Make sure to stay in school no matter how hard you think it may be. Also be sure to make sure you know who your real friends are. The ones that will encourage you to stay in school and follow your passion. Just do not give up and follow your dreams until they come through. Even if it takes time to study and work for. Maybe you want to play sports, and work until you can get a starting spot. Or even try to go to the majors. Do not give up, always try your hardest.

HANG TOUGH

No Matter How Hard

Lukas

Dear 9th graders,

Don't give up no matter how hard school is going to get. When school gets hard, always remember you've got friends to help you out along the way. You can also ask a teacher to help you out. The main thing that you don't want to happen is you get in trouble for doing something bad.

You can accomplish anything that you put your mind to.

The People You're Doing It For

Cordé

Stay in school and don't give up. If it gets hard, remember why you started. Think about all your loved ones—the people you're doing it for. Stay on task and don't hang with the wrong people. Stay focused.

To My Future Self

Zack

I am going to drive a nice car, have a good life, and make good grades. When I get old, me and my family will go out of town and have good jobs. I like art class.

All That Mess

Trin

Keep your grades up and don't get caught up in all of that mess. When you get your first car, don't let everyone ride with you.

    Try out for sports you always wanted to
        try out for.

    Don't be friends with just anyone.

    Try your best at everything you do.

The Right Crowd

Chakevious

Stay in school and get your education. Stick around with the right friend group who want to see you do better. Get better grades. Stay out of trouble. Do better for yourself.

It Goes by Fast

TC

Just behave and pay attention, because it goes by in a fly.
Stay ahead while you can.
Behave, because I heard they don't play over there in high school.
Stay above your grades so colleges will see you.
Set yourself up for the future.

CJ's Friend

Allen

No matter what, keep working hard, pass all your
    classes, and avoid fights.
You can achieve your dreams.
Hang out with people who will benefit you.
Stay friends with CF.
And most of all, avoid drugs, because all they will
    do is mess up your life.
Please don't get into fights with family members,
    or CJ.
That's all.
And whatever you do, never drop out.

To My 9th-Grade Self

Ja' Quinton

I'm gonna go to high school and continue
 to focus on my dream.
I would like to say I cannot be focused on
 anything but myself and making my
 mama proud.
I would love to be known my freshman
 year.
People know me for being positive, not
 negative.
I will go into freshman year prepared,
 focused, and ready to make good
 decisions and good grades.

Stay in School

Carsten

Stay in school and don't fail.
Don't drop out.
Keep your grades up, and pull girls.

Fresh Start

Kelly

So this is your 9th-grade year, a fresh start.
Just three more years and you're done.
Stay strong. Keep going no matter how hard it
    gets.
This just the beginning of life.
Nothing is worth stressing over.
On the first day, take all the stress and put it
    away.
You got this!

Stay Calm

Brody Storey

I'm a 7th grader at Calloway Middle
    School, and I want to say this:
Don't let things stop and stress you
    out—like gaming, relationships,
    grades.
Stay calm.
I know your friends and girls may get
    on your nerves.
Still, make sure you keep up your
    grades and focus on school
A lot of opportunities will come out of
    that.
Remember what is important.
Stay true to yourself.

My Hope

Chris Jung

I hope you stay in school and do the best you can.
Even if you're discouraged, keep going, never give up.
There are going to be hard times, in school and life.
But you have to keep going.
Make sure you avoid fights and drugs.
Avoid bad things at all costs, even if your friends try to
    convince you to do something bad.
Be considerate of your friends and family members.
Stay humble.
Help out as many people as you can.
Doing good things will come back to you.
Going into high school will be a big change.
But try your best, achieve your goals.

You'll Get By

Kae Kae

Life is going to be hard, but . . .
Stay in school and make good grades.
Be good, don't talk back to any teachers.
If someone is being a bully, tell an adult.
Don't hang around people who do bad things.
You'll get through it.

Never Say Never

JW

Never say never.
Study hard.
You're going to have a good job.
Work hard.
Never give up.

Push Forward,
Don't Hold Back

Alysiah

Stay in school, keep your grades up, and no smoking or
  drinking.
Don't hang with the wrong crowd.
No disrespecting your teacher.
Push yourself to do what you're supposed to do.
Do not have a baby at a young age, wait.
Do not try to be like your friends who are doing the
  wrong thing.
Just do yourself.
Push yourself, do not hold yourself back.

The Best Year

DK

I wish you the best year your first year of high school
with the best teachers and the best friends.
But don't forget about your grades.
And don't forget to have fun.
And don't stress, that's important.
Have fun your first year of high school
All the time.

Gratitude

Dr. Coach Griff

Wake up every day and be grateful.
Someone else has it worse.
Find them and be a helping hand.
Meet new people.
Build relationships.
You are fearless, move like it!

Smile more.
Hug your friends.
Tell your family you love them.
Pray.
Meditate.
Love.
Think positively.
The positivity you put out will return in greater forms.

Work hard when nobody is paying attention.
Be a self-starter.
Don't rely on others' confirmation.
Listen to your teachers,
One day they will have to sign a recommendation letter
    for you.

ADVICE TO 9TH GRADERS

Avoid peer pressure, drama, and negativity
At all costs.
Dare to be different.
Go outside more.
Travel and see the world.
Dream big and do the work needed.

Nothing will be given to you.
Work when they're sleeping.
Play sports.
Make a resumé.
Do dual enrollment.
Take the ACT/SAT.
Get your license.

Get out of your own way.
Find what pushes you and keep pushing!
Stop thinking so much.
Relax.
Grow.

The Contributors

Akinn Solis is an artist! "I love my family and friends, who are a great inspiration. I am a 15-year-old sophomore at Parkrose High School in Portland, Oregon."

Alphonsine Mbuyi is a junior and a POPS club member at Venice High School. A Black student, Alphonsine is also a member of the Black Student Achievement Program. An introvert, she writes poems; loves music, sports, singing, and dancing; and has been a member of the varsity dance team and the JV swimming team. She is Congolese, from the Democratic Republic of Congo, who came to America at age eight. She has five siblings.

AM is a 15-year-old girl at El Camino Real Charter High School. She loves music, travel, and playing the drums.

Amori Storms is a trans teen who wants people to understand differences and diversities and make others more comfortable in who they are and to be respectful of others.

THE CONTRIBUTORS

Andrea Phoebe Orduña is a beginner poet who expresses her thoughts and emotions through the flow of words. She is 15 years old and proceeds to write her book, describing her journey, pain, and progress through heartbreak.

Ashley Villatoro-Gomez is a 15-year-old sophomore at Culver City High who aspires to help others now and in her future career.

Avel is a poet who is trying to deal with and express her emotions through poetry. She believes everyone should try to express themselves in their own way, to know themselves, and to know they are not alone.

Billy Mendez Trujillo is an 11th grader at Venice High School. "I love art and always look for ways to express myself and help others. I feel that my art and my poetry can help others understand."

BL is a sophomore at Parkrose High. He is part of The PATHfinder Club at his school, and he wants to major in creative writing.

Bonnie Loborico is a 16-year-old girl who goes to Parkrose High School. She loves reading any type of book. She loves seeing everyone happy and safe.

Chelsea Robb is a freshman at New Village Girls Academy who has a strong passion for law and politics. She is a law intern at an immigration firm and is involved in programs that include youth and government. Chelsea is ambitious and determined and never backs down from a challenge.

She hopes to change the world through her passion for justice and the people.

Cherry is a sophomore at Los Angeles High School of the Arts. "This is my first year in POPS the Club. I'm 15 years old, and I live in Los Angeles, Koreatown!"

Daphne Colio is a sophomore at Los Angeles High School of the Arts. "The poem I wrote is about the school year in 9th grade, about how I started off good but almost ended bad. But luckily I kept pushing myself to do well. And I hope that other people do the same, so even if you somehow keep slipping, just push yourself a little harder and you'll get to where you want to be."

Davi M. R. Cavalcanti is an exchange student from Brazil at Parkrose High School. "I came from a modest family but they always gave me everything that they could, and I came to the USA to learn English and to try to get a scholarship here to be able to give a better life to my mom and the people I love. I hope I can bring my family to live here with me."

Dennis Danziger is the cofounder of POPS the Club, a 24-year veteran Los Angeles Unified School District English teacher, and coauthor (with John Rodriguez) of the memoir *Put Down Your Pistol and Pick Up a Pen*.

Donaji Garcia is a third-year college student at California State University, Northridge, once a POPS club member at Venice High. "I dedicate this work to my sister who is still in high school as well as the many umbrellas I have had in high school. Thanks for protecting me from the rain."

THE CONTRIBUTORS

Drake Witham is a special-education teacher in Los Angeles and sponsors the POPS club at Venice High School.

Estephanie Lopez is a POPS club member at El Camino Real Charter High School in Woodland Hills, California.

Feven B. is a 17-year-old girl who wants to figure out what to do after high school. "But I'm scared I'm going to fail and go down a wrong path. I worry I won't do the things I want to do and struggle to make a living or have fun doing what I like. I know there are many people like me who struggle to find themselves, and I want to help."

Giselle Montiel-Laconna is a junior at Venice High School. A multitalented artist/musician/writer, she speaks the truth of her cultural experiences as a first-generation Latina-American.

Gizella Huertas enjoys meeting new people, and POPS the Club has taught her a lot about the prison system and the pain that comes with it.

Hailey Garcia Garcia is a member of POPS the Club at Culver City High School, where she is a 9th grader. At POPS she feels supported and free to share her feelings without judgment.

Imari Stevenson is a POPS club graduate from Venice High School in Los Angeles. "Take your adventure step by step and live with no regrets."

JJ is an aspiring writer hoping to find and heal themself through writing and comedy. They are hoping to improve their spelling too.

Jaden Saetern is a 10th grader at Parkrose High School in Portland, Oregon. Jaden likes to cook and wants to get better at it.

Jess Sandoval is a 23-year-old now living in Portland, OR, and supports the facilitation of The PATHfinder Club. Jess has experienced the impacts that incarceration, detention, and deportation have on families and communities within her own home. Since she was a little girl, she always wished that things could be different for herself, and while some things can't be changed, she hopes to provide support to other youth silenced by the systems that silenced her.

Jimmie Harmon writes, "I had a dream once/I lived with you and we had a detective agency/I wanna do stupid things and solve crimes with you forever."

Jonathan Gonzalez is a junior at El Camino Real Charter High School in Woodland Hills, California.

Kai Salazar feels like the coolest person ever to be leading The PATHfinder Club at Parkrose High School. Kai enjoys advocating for her community and hanging out with her friends. She hopes to run for office and change the system from within.

Kavon Ray is a senior at Venice High School, a member of the basketball team, and a proud member of POPS.

Kay is a 16-year-old girl who attends El Camino Real High School. Growing up in Canoga Park to a single mother, she dedicates her work to the people she loves and has learned from the most. She loves getting lost in words.

Kennedy Johnson is a junior at Venice High School in Los Angeles.

Krystle May Statler lives as a daughter of incarcerated parents and a sister who suffers the unimaginable loss of her older brother, BJ, murdered by the Inglewood Police Department on March 27, 2019. She writes with and for BJ, turning to poetry to hold the weight of grief, honor healing, and explore what it means to live this brotherless life. Poetry keeps the door open as the safest path toward justice and keeps BJ alive every day.

KWL is a high school student based in Southern California. She enjoys writing, playing electric guitar, singing, dancing, practicing martial arts, and trying new food and hobbies. KWL is also involved in student government and leadership roles such as class president. After high school she would like to become an emergency room and/or family medical physician to help others and to create a better experience for all throughout the healthcare system.

Laine Riley is a senior at Venice High School who transferred there from Salt Lake City. She likes to crochet and sew, loves all kinds of music, and is passionate about the environment. She plans to study psychology in college. She loves trying new things and learning about different cultures.

Leo Acosta is a junior at Venice High School who is funny and likes to do a bunch of stuff with friends.

Lisbeth Vásquez is a member of the POPS club at Los Angeles High School of the Arts.

Lyric Farmer is 25 years old, a Libra at heart. "Even with a past of addiction, I am now a grateful recovering addict who is athletic and outgoing, and I love my cat. Poetry has always been a positive outlet for me, even for my darker thoughts. I strive to lead by example and to leave behind a story worth telling."

Malikiah Ozment is a POPS club member in Georgia with a troubled past and a prosperous future.

Maxwell Poll is a 16-year-old Ukrainian American of Jewish descent who enjoys technology, philosophy, and fitness, but more than anything learning and trying new things. Striving to be better every day, he wants his work to spread the message that logic, discipline, and discovery combined with passion and a love for one's fellow man are capable of changing the world.

Nathan Pugh was born on April 22, 2008, in Beverly Hills, California, to Nathan Pugh the 3rd and Jennene Pugh. Nathan has five brothers and sisters named Jiselle, Zella, Stacie, Journey, and Jazmine. "My name, Nathan, is Hebrew and means 'Gift of God.' I was named after my father and his father before him and his father before him. My family is special to me because I look like my father and my siblings, which causes me to be very close to them. I also love my pets, Jax and Sundae."

Nico Romero is a member of POPS the Club at Venice High School.

Nimran Singh is a sophomore at El Camino Real Charter High School who overcame mental health issues her freshman year and strives to reach out to others who may be struggling. She wants to raise awareness about mental health and help others.

NM is a strong, creative, funny person who wants to be a great business owner. NM wants to achieve all her goals in life and more. She is a girl who wants to change things in the world for good and will do anything to do so.

Oliver Green is a sophomore at El Camino Real Charter High School. "I enjoy reading, writing, and listening to music. Throughout high school, I've learned a lot about different activities and events, and I'm happy to be sharing my experiences with other interested students."

Owen Brookshire is a high school student and POPS club member in Georgia. Although he has a passion for cooking and making others laugh, he has a love-hate relationship with human interaction. As he lives his day-to-day life, he learns about resiliency, moving forward, making difficult decisions, and fighting for his best future.

Paulina Luke is a Ukrainian-American writer and comedian from Los Angeles, California.

Penmaneby Caerulea is a POPS the Club member at Robert Fitzgerald Kennedy Community Schools, Los Angeles High School of the Arts. She has a great passion for creative writing and literature.

Rachael Galper is a 16-year-old sophomore at El Camino Real Charter High School. She has a passion for photography, music, and dance. She strives to express her emotions and meaningful ideas through her art and to connect with people who may resonate with it.

Raymond Pacheco is 17 and enjoys the moment, loves to laugh, and is unpredictable.

RG is a member of The PATHfinder Club at Parkrose High. "I'm a very chill dude who is kind, caring, honest, gentle, and so much more. I play basketball and video games, and I love to draw. Any questions you want to ask I'll happily answer."

Roslyn Chamale is a 10th-grade student at Los Angeles High School of the Arts. She wants to share with upcoming 9th graders an artist who was very popular when she was in 9th grade, Mac Demarco, who wrote heartwarming songs that will get you through your day. She did her painting for someone special to her and is happy to enjoy it with you.

Sara Ivonne is a 16-year-old Mexican-American high school student who has recently gotten into writing poetry. Poetry is a gateway to letting her express her emotions and ideas.

Savannah Brewer is a junior at Venice High. She is Mexican-American, raised in a single-parent household. Savannah uses writing as a place to express her feelings.

Selma Bahy is a sophomore at El Camino Real Charter High School. "One thing I can truly assert about myself is that I'm a large extrovert. I have a lot of dreams and a lot of interests, and high school I think can take kids who are like me and help us flourish. I hope that my advice proves to be helpful to any student who may need or want a quick read."

Shakira Gomez is a member of POPS the Club at Los Angeles High School of the Arts.

Shay writes, "I like playing basketball and softball. I like reading a lot of books; it's like an escape. When I grow up, I want to be a lawyer to help people and defend them, just like I want to help people with my writing who might be struggling. It may sound corny, but I want to help make the world a better and fairer place!"

Stephanie Santiago Garcia is a freshman at New Village Girls Academy, a first-generation Mexican-American who has a passion for art.

Tamira Shany, a 16-year-old creator, thinker, and maker, spends most of her time focusing on science, technology, engineering, and mathematics but does find time for the arts. She attends El Camino Real Charter High School as a junior and strives for greatness.

Tyler Stonebraker is a high school student from Parkrose High who has been struggling with poverty all his life. He has had nobody to look up to but is trying to turn his life around and not live the lifestyle he has been living.

Valerie Contreras is a 17-year-old senior at Lawndale High School who aims to be a mechanical engineer and help make a difference in the STEM field for women.

Veda Mueller is a sophomore at Parkrose High School. "I am someone who loves art and have always tried to be creative. I have tried many forms of creativity, but drawing has always been my favorite. I have never known how to share my art, so this book is the start of my growth as an artist and as a person."

Victor Trillo Jr. experienced firsthand the enduring effects of incarceration. As a child and into his teenage years, his father was incarcerated. Vic yearned to go to prison because he wished to be with the father he so missed. When he himself was incarcerated, he experienced the anguish of being apart from his beloved daughter. Vic knows outlets exist for the pain and sorrow of children of the incarcerated, and he's overjoyed to be a pioneer of change and to have both his father and daughter in his life. "As the lead facilitator of The PATHfinder Club, I am humbled to sit in a space where instead of judgment there is community and support. I have so much gratitude for my freedom, my family, my beautiful daughter, and all the youth I mentor. In my spare time I love to relax, go for a ride in my car, and listen to music play very loudly while I dance and sing. I enjoy dressing nicely, wearing my favorite cologne, and I like to try different kinds of foods, though sandwiches are my favorite. I envision a brighter future where there is no shame and stigma attached to incarceration, deportation, and detention."

Will plays basketball and football, has friends, and plans to be successful and to work hard and play hard. "I love to go out with family and have a fun time and relax."

Yulissa Gonzalez is a 17-year-old Mexican-American artist. She grew up in Los Angeles, where her passion for art ignited. Art paved the way for her to embrace her Mexican heritage and envision stories that deserve to be told in her community. Yulissa expresses her creativity through a variety of artistic mediums—digital art, silkscreen, painting, and photography. Her artwork focuses on the visual storytelling of Black, Brown, and Indigenous people. Yulissa is determined to become a professional artist and attain a degree in illustration. She distributes her art throughout Los Angeles with her murals, stickers, and screen-printed shirts and tote bags. Her work has been highlighted by professional artists such as graphic designers at Nike, photo curators at Netflix, and animators from Discovery Channel.

Zaleeyah Ross is a member of POPS the Club at Culver City High, where she is a 10th grader.

The Callaway Kids

The students in POPS the Club at Callaway Middle School in Troup County, Georgia, are 6th, 7th, and 8th graders who shared their dreams and advice—both for themselves and for future 9th graders everywhere.

These are the Callaway writers:

Abby	Donovan
Akerria	DK
Alex	Dr. Coach Griff
Allen	e5lei
Alysiah	Emberily
Amiriyah	Emily
AP	Ethan
Bailee	Ja' Quinton
Bella	Jacob
Bradley	Jamal
Brody Storey	Jax
Brookelyn McGownse	Jaxsen Hudson
Bryson	Jaxon
Calleigh	JJ
Carsten	Jordan
Chakevious	JW
Chris Jung	KaeKae
Cookie	KaeKG
Cordé	Kelly
Corderiana	Kenny Jung
David	KWL

THE CONTRIBUTORS

Larry

Lukas

Maximus

Naya

Noah

Qua

Smoke

TC

Trin

Zack

Acknowledgments

F irst, we must say a huge thank-you to our angel donor, longtime champion of the publishing program and Out of the Woods Press, Madge Woods. This book is possible because of you. Thank you for your unwavering commitment to keeping the stories and the voices uplifted.

To the many donors who have supported our work, thank you; we are thriving with your support.

We are moved and forever amazed by the resilience, spirit, wisdom, courage, and generosity of the youth we have the honor to serve.

We wish to thank all who contributed to this volume, including current club members and graduates as well as friends of The PATHfinder Club and POPS the Club.

Of course, this book would not be possible without the leadership and guidance of the teachers, counselors, principals, and volunteers at our school clubs across the country. Thank you:

Parkrose High School Principal Molly Ouche, Vice Principal Kenneth Keyes and former Vice Principal Andre

Goodlow, and PATHfinder Club leaders Victor Trillo, Jr., Jess Sandoval, and chef Kristin Stoneberg.

Bronx Academy of Letters, thank you to Principal Amy Schless and to teacher sponsor Michael Alston.

Callaway Middle School, Troup County, Georgia, thank you to Principal McRae and to Community in Schools POPS club leader Dr. Nicholas Griffin.

Culver City High School in Culver City, California, thank you to club sponsor Catherine Lenke and volunteer Ann Kelly. And sincere thanks to the chefs, staff, and owner Teri Ernst of Dinah's Family Restaurant in Los Angeles for the delicious lunches they provide each week to POPS club members.

El Camino Real Charter High School in Woodland Hills, California, thank you to School Director David Hussey and teacher sponsors James DeLarme, Nicholas Schulyer, counselor Xenia Paniagua, and volunteers Katie Kritzell and Chloe Parker.

Gardner Newman Middle School, Troup County, Georgia, thank you to Principal Kelley Adams and Community in Schools POPS club leader Trenton Huzzie.

Los Angeles High School of the Arts in Los Angeles, thank you to POPS club founding principal Susan Canjura, Principal Cathy Kwan, teacher sponsor Elizabeth Mora, and volunteer Casey Velasquez. Thank you too to the chefs, staff, and owners Fernando, Bricia, and Elizabeth Lopez of Guelaguetza Restaurante in Los Angeles for the delicious lunches you provide POPS club members each week.

Lawndale High School in Los Angeles, thank you to Principal Anjelica Mejia and teacher sponsors Reza Mir, Michelle Howard, and Tuan Hophan.

Long Cane Middle School, Troup County, Georgia, thank you to Principal Whitney Glisson and Community in Schools POPS club leader Frederick Stanley.

McDonough High School in McDonough, Georgia, thank you to Principal McRae, Vice Principal Mikal Underwood, and Community in Schools POPS club leader Kara Colley.

New Village Girls Academy in Los Angeles, thank you to Principal Jennifer Quinones and club sponsor Kyle Denman.

Stockbridge High School, Stockbridge, Georgia, Henry County, thank you to Principal Dr. James Thornton and to Community in Schools POPS club leader Kathleen Richardson.

At Venice High School in Los Angeles, thank you to Principal Cynthia Headrick and to teacher sponsors Drake Witham and Alejandro Arroyo and POPS the Club cofounder and volunteer Dennis Danziger.

Thank you to Communities in Schools Georgia administrators Tabitha Coverson, Nichole Tigner, and Denise Wright.

We also wish to thank Dr. Myriam Forster, associate professor of public health at California State University, Northridge, and her team members Lizbeth Becerra, Yanira Casasola, Stephanie Donis, Maria Guevara, Lydia Lising, Mariana Garcia Martinez, Michael Mitchell, Velia Nunez, Suzette Quijada, Cynthia Robles, Kim Rogers, Mikaela Rojas, Sabikun Nahar Satil, Eric Shanazari, Jazmine Victoria, and Jonathan Watts, for their diligence and passion in leading their multiyear NIH-funded study (SHARE) examining the effect of the support we provide to our youth.

ACKNOWLEDGMENTS

Sincere thanks to the staff of The Pathfinder Network for carrying out the mission of our agency in such powerful and transformative ways. Heartfelt thanks to our executive leadership team Sheri Sandoval, Jennifer Beck, Lainie Watson, and Krystle May Statler for always showing up and making it happen. Much gratitude to our Mentoring Inside Out youth mentoring team for seeding and inspiring our work. To our board of directors: Dr. Mauri Matsuda (president), Alissa Skog (secretary), Mary Stephenson Scott (treasurer), as well as Zach Winston, Noah Morss, Chad Marting, Marcia Kadanoff, Michael Saenz, Alycia Bleeker, and Marquita Jaramillo, thank you for your continued support as POPS became a part of TPN and as we expand and grow. With your belief in the importance of this work and the artistry of the young people we serve, this book is possible.

We invite you to dive into these pages and come to know the people who have changed our lives for the better.

—Leticia Longoria-Navarro, Executive Director,
The Pathfinder Network
—Amy Friedman, Cofounder and Editor, POPS the
Club and Out of the Woods Press

"Our Secret Garden," Dennis Danziger